Link it!

Masterpieces of Bridge Design

Chris van Uffelen

Link it!

Masterpieces of Bridge Design

BRAUN

CONTENTS

- 6 **PREFACE**

- 8 **SAMUEL BECKETT BRIDGE**
  Santiago Calatrava

- 14 **LINDLINGALM SUSPENSION BRIDGE**
  Erhard Kargel

- 20 **REGGIO EMILIA PONTI**
  Santiago Calatrava

- 24 **GARDEN OF 10,000 BRIDGES**
  West 8 urban design & landscape architecture

- 28 **TRAUNSTEG MUSEUM ANGERLEHNER**
  Erhard Kargel

- 34 **WUPPERBRÜCKE**
  Ercan Ağırbaş Friends, Wienstroer Architekten Stadtplaner

- 40 **KAZIMIERZ LUDWINÓW PEDESTRIAN BRIDGE**
  Biuro Projektów Lewicki Łatak

- 44 **OSTHAFENBRÜCKE AND HONSELLBRÜCKE**
  Ferdinand Heide Architekt

- 48 **WEYMOUTH BRIDGE**
  Bruce Williams

- 52 **HYDRASPAN**
  Future Cities Lab, Nataly Gattegno + Jason Kelly Johnson

- 56 **VIADUC DE MILLAU**
  Foster + Partners

- 60 **MÜHLENINSEL BRIDGE**
  Kolb Ripke Architekten

- 64 **PEDESTRIAN AND BICYCLE BRIDGE, KIEV**
  Leuppi & Schafroth Architekten

- 68 **PONT JEAN-JACQUES BOSC**
  OMA

- 72 **HOVENRING**
  ipv Delft

- 78 **ALFRED-LION-STEG**
  Kolb Ripke Architekten

- 82 **PASSERELLE SIMONE-DE-BEAUVOIR**
  Dietmar Feichtinger Architectes

- 86 **TRAUNSTEIN BRIDGE ENSEMBLE**
  Richard J. Dietrich Büro für Ingenieur-Architektur

- 90 **WALDSCHLÖSSCHEN-BRÜCKE**
  Kolb Ripke Architekten

- 94 **ENNIGER BRIDGE**
  Pirmin Jung Ingenieure für Holzbau

- 100 **BRIDGE SCHOOL**
  Li Xiaodong/atelier

- 104 **ELASTIC PERSPECTIVE**
  Next architects

- 110 **KIRCHENBRÜCKE**
  Eduard Imhof, Architekt

- 114 **HIGHWAY BRIDGE, WÜRZBURG**
  Richard J. Dietrich Büro für Ingenieur-Architektur

- 118 **PHYLLIS J. TILLEY MEMORIAL FOOTBRIDGE**
  Rosales + Partners

- 124 **AARSCHOT PEDESTRIAN BRIDGE**
  West 8 urban design & landscape architecture

- 128 **NA DRUK GELUKBRUG**
  René van Zuuk Architects

- 134 **UPSIDE DOWN BRIDGE**
  nooyoon by Hyuntek Yoon

- 138 **STÖRBRÜCKE**
  Winking · Froh Architekten

- 140 **PEACE BRIDGE**
  Santiago Calatrava

- 146 **HELIX BRIDGE**
  Cox Architecture, Architects 61

- 150 **BRIDGE OF STRINGS**
  Santiago Calatrava

- 154 **SEELE GLASS BRIDGE**
  IBK Forschung + Entwicklung

- 158 **WOVEN BRIDGE**
  MLRP Architecture, research and development

- 162 **GREEN SCHOOL MILLENIUM BRIDGE**
  Ibuku

- 166 **WAVEDECKS**
  West 8 urban design & landscape architecture

- 170 **MONKEY BRIDGE**
  Olivier Grossetête

- 174 **BOUNCING BRIDGE**
  AZC

- 180 **MELKWEGBRIDGE**
  Next architects

- 186 **ELB BRIDGE U-BAHN STATION**
  gmp Architekten von Gerkan, Marg und Partner

- 190 **MAX-GLEISSNER-BRÜCKE**
  Annabau Architektur und Landschaft, Moritz Schloten

- 196 **D-SPLINE**
  ONL [Oosterhuis_Lénárd]

- 202 **SCHERKONDETALBRÜCKE**
  Ingenieurbüro Marx Krontal, DB ProjektBau, Büchting + Streit, Stephan Sonnabend

- 206 **INDEX**

PREFACE

Bridges have existed longer than humanity. At some point in the depths of time a tree fell over a stream and became a bridge. Our ancestors saw it, copied it and thus the bridge became, in all likelihood, one of the first manmade constructions. Later, bridge decks were built of stone and at some point a supporting middle column was added so that gaps of longer distances could be bridged (Clapper Bridge in Postbridge, Dartmoor). The first suspension bridges were built in Asia and Africa as early as the Bronze Age; while the arch bridge was invented in Mesopotamia.

At this time, Ancient Greece was still reliant upon a straight rather than arch design, which made it impossible for them to build high, long bridges. Under the Romans, bridge design progressed in leaps and bounds. The development of stone arch bridges (Pont du Gard, Nîmes, 14 AD) made it possible to build bridges pretty much anywhere. The first rope bridge was built in China in around the second century AD; followed approximately three hundred years later by iron chain bridges.

In the Middle Ages ancient bridges were still used, but important new constructions were also built, such as the Pont d'Avignon (1188) and the London Bridge (1209). Bridge towers became an important part of the construction, for example those erected by Peter Parler on the Charles Bridge in Prague (begun in 1357). The gates through the towers – and sometimes bridge tolls – strengthened the sense of a boundary between the road and the bridge. Individual buildings in the center of the bridge, such as bridge chapels popular in the Middle Ages, emphasize the special situation of the bridge as a location rather than just an extension of the road and a means by which to cross the river.

'Living bridges', with buildings on either side along the entire length of the bridge, like the Ponte Vecchio in Florence (1345), have a very different character: one hardly recognizes the fact that one is crossing a river. This kind of bridge not only connects two city districts, it adds an urban accent that fuses two areas together. The bridges over the Seine in Paris also served a commercial purpose, although the oldest of these that still remains today – the Pont Neuf (1578–1607, Baptiste et Jacques II Androuet du Cerceau, F. des Isles, G. Marchand, T. Métezeau) – was the first to be built without such commercial buildings, as these would have blocked views of the Louvre, which at that time was still the Royal Palace. The Pont Neuf, 238 meters long and 20 meters wide, connects the two banks of the Seine and rests in the middle on the Île de la Cité. This was an inspirational role model for advancing bridge development.

In 1669 Louis XIV named Jean-Baptiste Colbert as the first official commissioner for bridge and road construction, which led to the development of the world's first engineering school during the Age of Enlightenment: The educational model at the École des Ponts et Chaussées (1747) was based on an increasing knowledge of physics. The work of the school's first director Jean-Rodolphe Perronet, for example what is today known as the Pont de la Concorde in Paris (1786–1791), was seen as an affront against academic architecture. The age-long rivalry between architects and engineers can be traced back to the "farther of modern architecture".

It was at this time that iron was also being developed as a building material (cast iron bridge Coalbrookdale, 1779). In the 19th century, bridge construction became more professional, thanks to the influence of engineering schools and public officers (e.g. construction inspector Thomas Telford; building surveyor Karl Friedrich Schinkel). Numerous bridges were built for the railway (Britannia Bridge over the Menai Strait, 1850), Gustave Eiffel perfected prefab construction (Douro-Bridge, Porto, 1877) and the dimensions increased enormously. Highlights include the Firth of Forth Bridge (Scotland, 1889, picture) as well as the Brooklyn Bridge (New York City, 1883).

Steel replaced cast iron and made the construction of much bolder suspension bridges possible (Golden Gate Bridge, San Francisco, 1937). Reinforced concrete has also been used increasingly since the beginning of the 20th century. The pioneers of reinforced concrete, François Hennebique (Wiggen, 1894), Robert Maillart (Salginatobel Bridge, 1928–1930) and Eugène Freyssinet (five bridges over the Marne, 1947–1951) made good use of this material.

By this time bridge construction needed to accommodate heavy traffic and must be able to bear more weight than ever before. Towards the mid-20th century pre-stressed concrete bridges were primarily used for bridge construction. Since then, the ongoing race for building faster and higher and pushing the boundaries more than ever before led to new problems and solutions. In contrast to the earlier focus on the more functional aspects of bridge architecture, today's bridges display a greater esthetic value.

This volume demonstrates a wide variety of different bridge types that don't just concern themselves with the 'getting over' a river or any other kind of obstacle, but that also connect the bridge with the surrounding context.

Commissioned by Dublin City Council, the Samuel Beckett Bridge (formerly Macken Street Bridge) is one of the two bridges in Dublin designed by Calatrava, the other being the James Joyce Bridge completed in 2003. Calatrava's Samuel Beckett Bridge features four lanes, two for traffic with cycle tracks and pedestrian paths on either side, as well as room for trams; to be implemented in the future. This cable-stayed balanced bridge with two unequal spans provides vehicular traffic and pedestrian access crossing the Liffey River. To avoid disturbing maritime traffic, Calatrava also designed the bridge with the ability to rotate 90 degrees horizontally, enabling ships to pass.

SAMUEL BECKETT BRIDGE
DUBLIN, IRELAND

Architects: Santiago Calatrava
Structural engineers: Santiago Calatrava
Location: Macken Street/Cardiff Lane and Guild Street, Dublin, Ireland
Length: 124 m
Completion: 2009
Client: Dublin City Council
Bridge type: cable-stayed balanced swing bridge

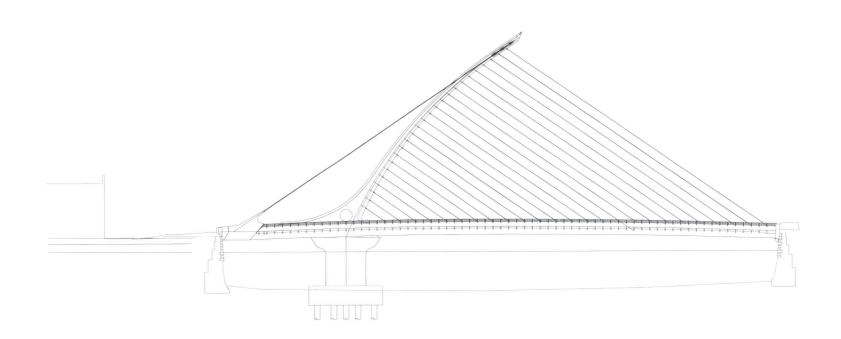

"Love is the bridge between you and everything."
– Rumi, Persian poet

Architect: Erhard Kargel
Structural engineers: Erhard Kargel, Hans Wagner/ABES
Steel construction: Oberhofer Stahlbau
Location: Talschlussweg 367, 5754 Hinterglemm, Austria
Length: 200 m
Completion: 2010
Client: Reinhold Bauböck, Bartl Hasenauer
Bridge type: suspension bridge

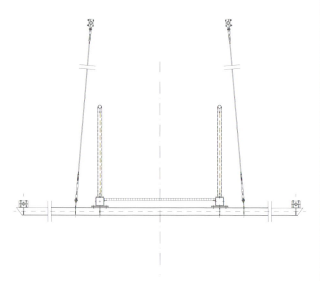

LINDLINGALM SUSPENSION BRIDGE
HINTERGLEMM, AUSTRIA

This suspension bridge at the head of the Glemm Valley, 1,300 meters above sea level, was commissioned by two private clients: a restaurant owner and the operator of a treetop path. They were unable to use public grants to fund the construction; therefore, it was important that the bridge attained maximum effect with minimum expenditure, both in terms of economical factors and the design itself. Two pylons support the suspension cables and are built at different heights in order to suit the topography. Two pre-stressed cables are fitted to either side of the bridge deck and help to stabilize the entire system. The steel grating suspended 40 meters above the Saalach is, for some, a test of nerves.

The Golden Gate Bridge in San Francisco, has a total length of 2,737 meters and features 129,000 kilometers of wire in its two main cables.

Architects: Santiago Calatrava
Structural engineers: Santiago Calatrava
Location: Viale Trattati di Roma, Reggio nell'Emilia, Italy
Length: 221 and 179 m
Completion: 2007
Client: Municipality of Reggio Emilia and Treno Alta Velocità (TAV)
Bridge type: arched and cable-stayed bridges

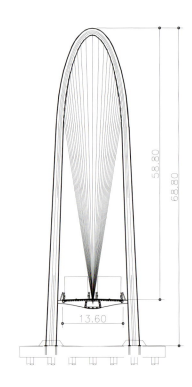

REGGIO EMILIA PONTI
REGGIO EMILIA, ITALY

In October 2007, an ensemble of three arched and cable-stayed bridges was inaugurated in Reggio Emilia, as the first part of a larger infrastructure project. Plans for the bridges originated in 2002, when a new railway station was designed. In addition, a master plan for the surrounding areas of the city was created, to improve access to the site and provide an impressive new entrance from the north. This plan called for adding three new bridges to the station area, designed to connect the Autostrada del Sole (A1) to the city by a multi-lane highway. The two high arches create the appearance of a towering gate marking the entrance to the city.

"A modern bridge can also be a work of art, helping to shape not only the landscape but also the daily lives of the people who use it." — Santiago Calatrava, Spanish architect, engineer, artist

Architects: West 8 urban design & landscape architecture
Structural engineers: West 8 urban design & landscape architecture
Location: Xi'an International Horticultural Expo, Guangyun Lake, Xi'an, China
Length: 12 m
Completion: 2011
Client: International Horticulture Exhibition 2011
Bridge type: arched bridges

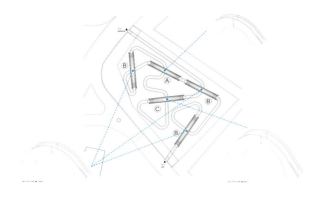

GARDEN OF 10,000 BRIDGES
XI'AN, CHINA

Gardens tell stories; they are like poetry and have a narrative. This garden represents the human condition, the path of people's lifetime. The Garden of 10,000 Bridges plays with perspective views, the idea of limits and the sensation of surprise. The path through the garden has only one entrance and one exit, curling through the garden of bamboo and passing over and under each bridge. The visitor cannot see where in the garden he or she is located or how much progress has been made. The bridges draws inspiration from China's rich history and translates it into a contemporary architectural language that is realized using modern construction techniques.

24 >> 25

The Zhaozhou Bridge is the oldest standing bridge in China and the world's oldest stone segmental arch bridge. Built in 605 AD, it is still standing strong today, over 1,400 years later.

Architect: Erhard Kargel
Structural engineers: Erhard Kargel,
Hans Wagner/ABES
Steel construction: Oberhofer Stahlbau
Light artist: Waltraut Cooper
Location: Ascheter Straße 54, 4600 Thalheim bei Wels, Austria
Length: 90 m
Completion: 2013
Client: Museum Angerlehner for the
municipalities of Wels and Thalheim
Bridge type: cantilever and girder bridge

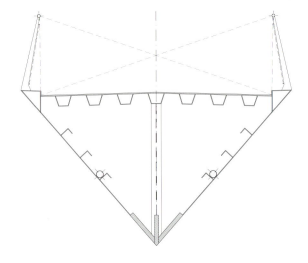

TRAUNSTEG MUSEUM ANGERLEHNER
WELS AND THALHEIM, AUSTRIA

The Traunsteg is a defining element on the route between the Wels trade fair buildings and Kunstmuseum Angerlehner. The slim bridge is 90 meters long and spans the River Traun without intermediate supports. It is constructed as a triangular box girder from steel. The height of the triangle increases from 1.00 to 2.25 meters at the center of the span. Despite its slender shape, no vibration dampers are necessary. The cross section is robust, torsionally rigid and has the smallest surface and number of edges possible. Artistically designed LED strips are integrated into the handrail.

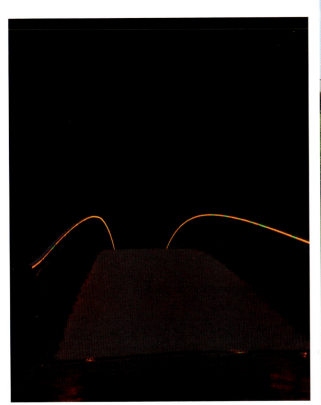

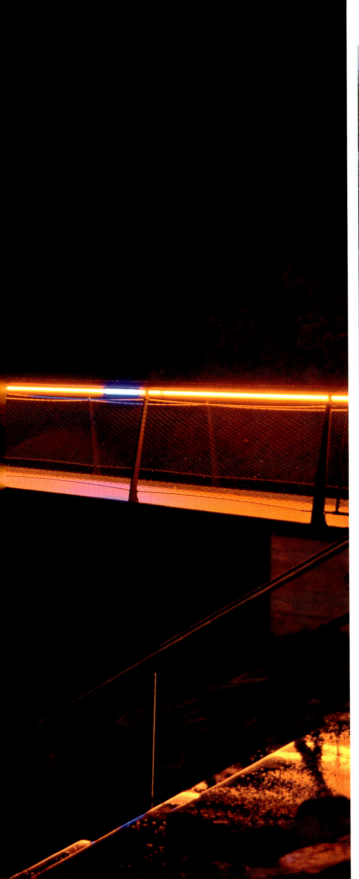

"Of everything that man erects and builds in his urge for living nothing is in my eyes better and more valuable than bridges." — Ivo Andrić, Serbian novelist

WUPPERBRÜCKE
LEVERKUSEN, GERMANY

Just like the existing bridge before it, which had to be demolished due to its age and resulting structural weaknesses, this new bridge has a modest appearance and is designed to subtly introduce new colors and character to the green park landscape. The steel sections of the bridge that meet the riverbanks on both sides are solid steel; this enables the rest of the bridge to span the river using as little material as possible. As a whole, the design plays with the contrast between light and heavy, a dialogue of dark and light, thick and thin, big and small. Directly above the river, pedestrian walk across a steel grid, with the water just below their feet. The bridge doesn't just serve as a convenient way to cross the river, it also features a bench, inviting passersby to linger and watch the water below.

Architects: Ercan Ağırbaş Friends, Wienstroer Architekten Stadtplaner
Structural engineers: Schüßler-Plan Ingenieurgesellschaft
Location: Ludwig-Rehbock-Anlage, Opladen, Leverkusen, Germany
Length: 72 m
Completion: 2012
Client: TBL, Technische Betriebe Leverkusen, Ulrich van Acken
Bridge type: cantilever and girder bridge

"A river seems a magic thing.
A magic, moving, living part of the very earth itself." –
Laura Gilpin, American photographer

KAZIMIERZ LUDWINÓW PEDESTRIAN BRIDGE
KRAKOW, POLAND

This footbridge is formed by three independent bands: two exterior bands with an arch profile and one middle band in the shape of a sinusoid. The cross section of each band is changeable. It is a steel structure created by mutually strengthening flat sheets to form bands joined together with bars. On the side of Kazimierz the two outer bands change in shape, giving the bridge a dynamic and unusual appearance. The bridge is supported by a reinforced steel construction with two steel pillars. On the Ludwinów side, the outer bands end at the abutments hidden in the earthy banks of the access roads.

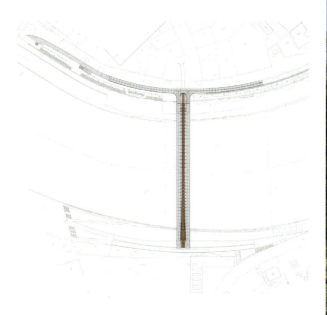

Architects: Biuro Projektów Lewicki Łatak
Structural engineers: Mosty Wrocław
Location: Kazimierz, Ludwinów - districts, Vistula River, Krakow, Poland
Length: 140 m
Design completion: 2011
Client: City of Krakow
Bridge type: cantilever and girder bridge

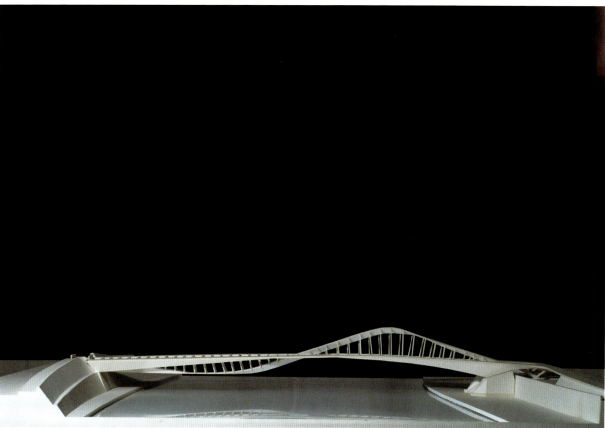

"In the moment of crisis, the wise build bridges and foolish build dams." – Nigerian proverb

Architects: Ferdinand Heide Architekt
Structural engineers: Grontmij Gmbh
Location: Frankfurt Ostend, Frankfurt/Main, Germany
Length: 175 m
Completion: 2013
Client: City of Frankfurt/Main
Bridge type: steel-arch bridge with suspended deck

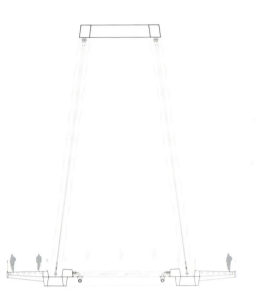

OSTHAFENBRÜCKE AND HONSELL-BRÜCKE
FRANKFURT/MAIN

The new Osthafenbrücke and Honsellbrücke complete each other, forming a harmonious unity. The original design concept from 1907 has been remodeled into a modern construction. The form, structure and materiality of the bridge seek to harmonize with the surroundings, the Honsellbrücke and the famous shell roof of Martin Elsässer's Wholesale Market Hall. The new bridge is less a construction that tries to draw attention to itself, and more a building block within an independent building ensemble in this industrial area. The Mainbrücke East connects two attractive zones along the riverbank with a series of urban spaces. The new design offers routes for cyclists and people simply taking a weekend stroll.

In the 1960s a part of the Mae Klong river in Thailand was renamed Kwai Yai because of the number of tourists looking for the bridge on the River Kwai.

Artist: Bruce Williams
Structural engineers: Dorset Engineering Consultancy
Location: Newstead Road, Weymouth, United Kingdom
Length: 60 m
Client: Dorset County Council and Sustrans cycling charity
Bridge type: three-span steel bridge

WEYMOUTH BRIDGE
WEYMOUTH, UNITED KINGDOM

2010 Bruce Williams' design for Weymouth Bridge emerged from two years of consultation with local residents. The result is that all the elements have been imbued with meaning. The span of the bridge is supported at two points by two very different column arrangements. The southern, Portland-end is a solid structure, clad with gabion cages, filled with Portland stone. The northern end is a collection of slender, asymmetrical masts that connect with the near-by marina and bring buoyancy to the structure. The modular, billowing steel railings on either side of the bridge have many echoes for Weymouth; the twisted fibers of maritime ropes, the steam clouds of trains that once followed this route or billowing sails.

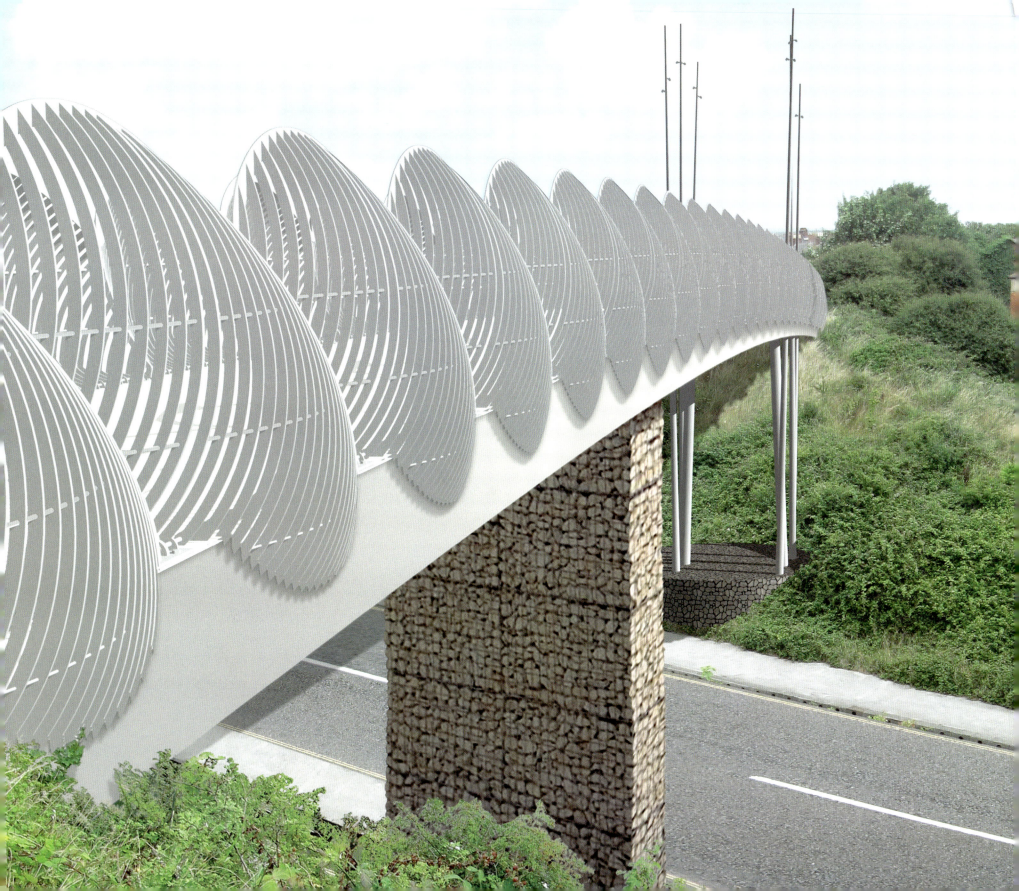

"As the wise man looks for a bridge the fool crosses the river." —
Persian proverb

Architects: Future Cities Lab, Nataly Gattegno + Jason Kelly Johnson
Location: San Francisco, Oakland Bay Bridge, CA, USA
Length: 3,000 m
Bridge type: suspension bridge

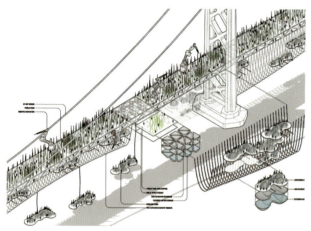

HYDRASPAN
SAN FRANCISCO, CA, USA

Hydraspan is a speculative proposal for the radical reuse and re-colonization of the San Francisco-Oakland Bay Bridge infrastructure. Suspended from the bridge trusses, thousands of fog-catching catenary ribbons sustain an inner world of domestic and agricultural activity: floating living units are tethered alongside fresh water catch basins, robotic sky pods support suspended fish farm vitrines, and the bridge trusses serve as the catalysts for social, political and commercial exchange. The speculative proposal was prototyped as a model exhibited at the Yerba Buena Center for the Arts in San Francisco 2013.

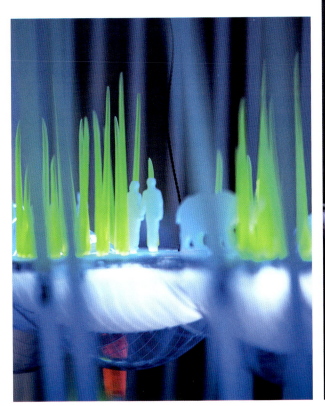

On the island of Sumatra, the two villages Pulut-pulut and Lubuak Glare are connected by the roots of a tree that acts as a bridge over the Bayang river. It is three meters long and one meter wide.

This bridge creates a direct route from Paris to Barcelona by crossing the River Tarn gorge. The cable-stayed, mast-supported structure is delicate and transparent with an optimum span between columns (342 meters). They range in height from 75 meters to 245 meters (taller than the Eiffel Tower), with the masts rising a further 87 meters above the road deck. Each column splits into two thinner more flexible columns below the roadway, forming an A-frame above deck level. The tapered form of the columns both expresses their structural loads and minimizes their profile. This gives the bridge a dramatic silhouette and, more crucially, minimizes intervention of the landscape.

VIADUC DE MILLAU
MILLAU, FRANCE

Architects: Foster + Partners
Length: 2,460 m
Completion: 2005
Client: French Ministry of Equipment, Transport, Housing, Tourism and Sea
Bridge type: cable-stayed

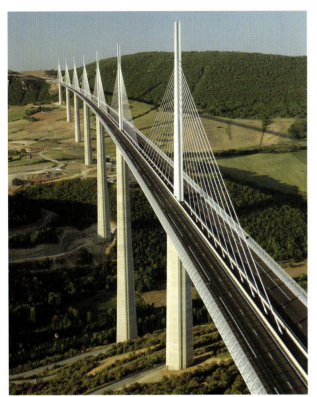

"Rivers flow not past, but through us; tingling, vibrating, exciting every cell and fiber in our bodies, making them sing and glide." – John Muir, Scottish-American naturalist

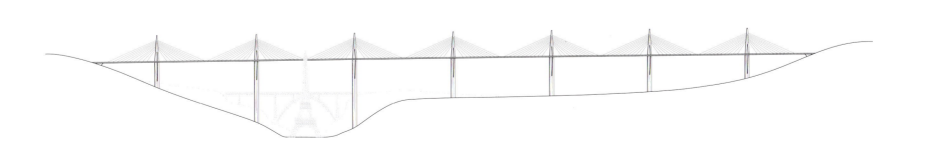

MÜHLENINSEL BRIDGE
KÖNIGS WUSTERHAUSEN, GERMANY

The design for this bridge was conceived as a fundamental part of the existing landscape. It extends the existing path and creates a new route over the river. Based on the guiding principle of "connecting to the landscape", the bridge was given a S-shape, corresponding to the meandering paths on the Mühleninsel. A second S-shape defines two 'stages', one above the canal and one in the park. From these two points, visitors have a good view of the surrounding landscape. Folding chairs are also available for anyone who wants to sit and enjoy the peaceful location. The platform over the Nottekanal is set back from the bridge deck, providing a protected space that invites passersby to linger.

Architects: Kolb Ripke Architekten
Structural engineers: BDC Dorsch Consult Ingenieurgesellschaft
Length: 33 m
Completion: 2013
Client: Amt für Stadtentwicklung, Sachgebiet Tiefbau Königs Wusterhausen
Bridge type: cantilever and girder bridge

"A bridge has no allegiance to either side." –
Les Coleman, British artist

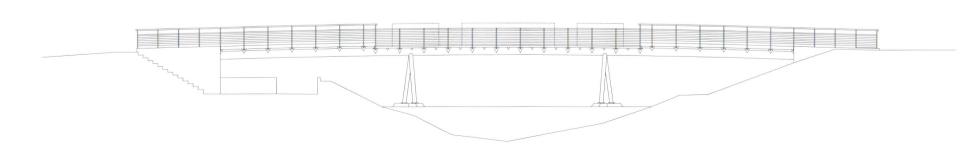

Located in the heart of the city of Kiev, just 500 meters from Maidan Square, this new pedestrian and bicycle bridge creates a connection between two parks — Khreshchatyi and Volodymyrska Hirka — that are interrupted by the Volodymyrski Uzviz thoroughfare. This elevated promenade is a logical continuation of the existing crest route through the uptown area and the Dnieper hills. Spanning the undulating topography with a nearly horizontal line, the bridge is conceived as a viaduct that quietly curves through the landscape. The configuration of the path directs views to the spectacular surroundings while preserving the protected park landscapes.

PEDESTRIAN AND BICYCLE BRIDGE
KIEV, UKRAINE

Architects: Leuppi & Schafroth Architekten
Structural engineers: Gruner + Wepf Ingenieure
Location: Parks Volodymyrska Hirka and Khreshchatyi, Kiev, Ukraine
Length: 213 m
Client: Kiev City Council, Department of Urban Development and Architecture
Bridge type: cantilever and girder bridge

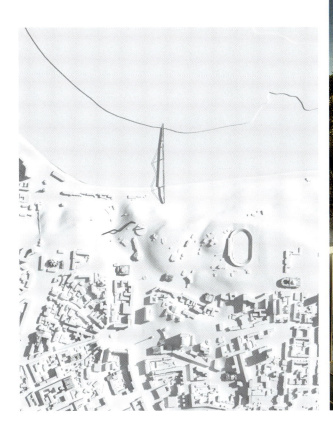

"Nobody can build the bridge for you to walk across the river of life, no one but you yourself alone." — Friedrich Nietzsche, German philosopher

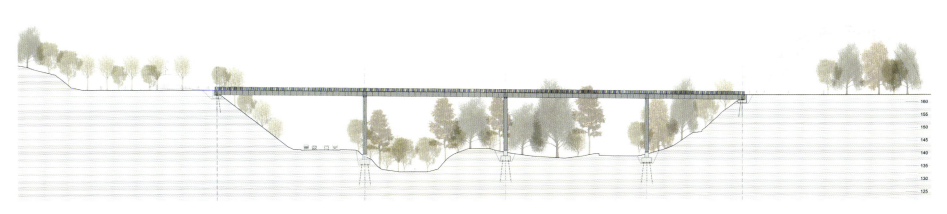

PONT JEAN-JACQUES BOSC
BORDEAUX, FRANCE

Positioned at the heart of the Euratlantique project, Pont Jean-Jacques Bosc provides a link between the municipalities of Bègles and Floriac. But more than simply connecting two points of land separated by water, the bridge itself also offers a generous new public space in the city. The gently sloping surface can accommodate a pedestrian promenade while still allowing the necessary clearance for boats beneath. All traffic modes — including private cars, public transport, bicycles and foot traffic — are accommodated by the width of the bridge, with the largest allowance devoted to pedestrians. The project was developed in collaboration with engineers WSP, landscape architect Michel Desvigne, and light design agency Lumières Studio.

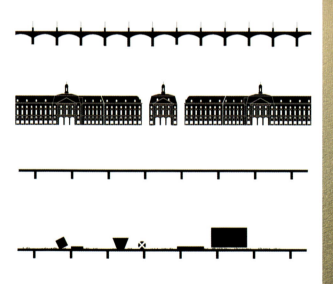

Architects: OMA Rem Koolhaas – Clement Blanchet
Structural engineers: WSP
Location: Bègles/Floriac, Bordeaux, France
Length: 545 m
Completion: 2018
Client: Committee of Bordeaux
Bridge type: cantilever and girder bridge

"A good person is more reliable than a stone bridge." —
Marc Aurel, Roman emperor

événement ponctuel

cinéma en plein-air

marché | tour de france / parade

Fête du vin

concert / festival

The Hovenring is a spectacular circular cycle bridge in the Dutch city of Eindhoven. The cable-stayed bridge hovers above the intersection like a flying saucer. With its impressive pylon, 72-meter diameter, thin deck and conspicuous lighting, the cyclist roundabout is a new landmark for the city. Ipv Delft had a very clear view of what the bridge should look like: a thin circular bridge deck and a powerfully shaped pylon. This required the creation of a lot of tailor-made solutions during the engineering phase. To allow for comfortable slopes for cyclists and pedestrians, the ground level of the intersection was lowered by a meter and a half.

HOVENRING
EINDHOVEN, THE NETHERLANDS

Architects: ipv Delft
Structural engineers: Witteveen+Bos
Location: Heerbaan/Noord-Brabantlaan, Eindhoven, The Netherlands
Diameter: 72 m
Completion: 2012
Client: Eindhoven City Council
Bridge type: cable-stayed bridge

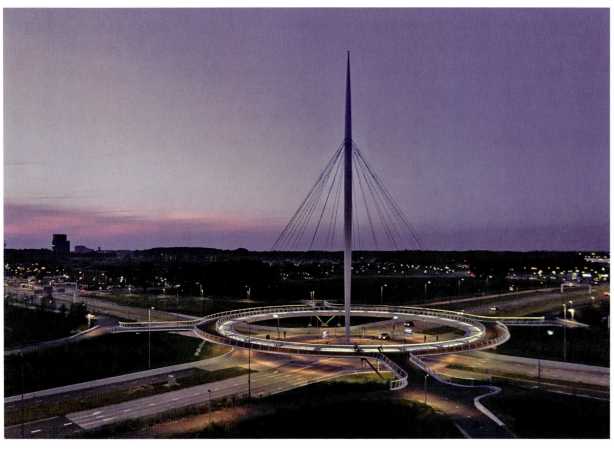

"There can be little doubt that in many ways the story of bridge building is the story of civilisation. By it we can readily measure an important part of a people's progress." –
Franklin D. Roosevelt, American president

A series of connected green areas have been created in the Tempelhof-Schöneberg district within the framework of the program "town renovation west". This new bridge for pedestrians and cyclists uses ramps and stairs to cross above the train tracks and connect residential areas. The construction comprises steel trusses that lean inwards to form a trapeze-shape cross-section. A handrail has been incorporated into the supporting structure and features integrated lighting. The trusses are gray and swing up in the middle and give the bridge a strikingly dynamic character. The design is a unique and characteristic component in the newly developed green zones linking the various residential areas.

ALFRED-LION-STEG
BERLIN, GERMANY

Architects: Kolb Ripke Architekten
Structural engineers: VIC - Brücken und Ingenieurbau
Location: Berlin-Schöneberg, Berlin, Germany
Length: 93 m
Completion: 2012
Client: Senatsverwaltung für Stadtentwicklung Berlin, Department X Ingenieurbauwerke
Bridge type: truss bridge

The Boston University Bridge is the only place in the world where a boat can sail under a train driving under a car driving under an airplane.

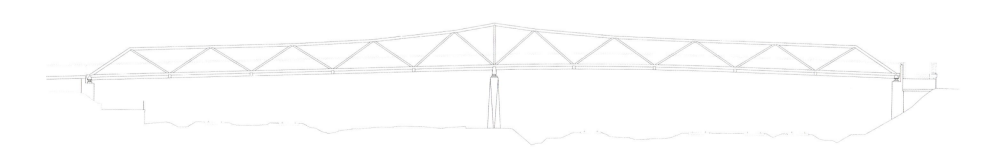

The pedestrian bridge with a width of twelve meters and an overall length of 304 meters connects the French National Library and the Bercy Park. Two curves create the geometry of the bridge, and their soft shape contrasts with the surrounding buildings. The combination of the upgoing – compressed – arc and the inversed – tensioned – arc enable the free span of 194 meters. The overlay of the two curves creates a lens formed space in the middle of the bridge, a public area suspended over the water. The multiple crossing options following the curves of the structure lead the pedestrians close to the water or allow a panoramic view over Paris.

PASSERELLE SIMONE-DE-BEAUVOIR
PARIS, FRANCE

Architects: Dietmar Feichtinger Architectes
Structural engineers: RFR
Length: 304 m
Completion: 2006
Client: Municipality of Paris
Bridge type: arched and suspension bridge

A "Bridge to nowhere" is a bridge standing alone in the landscape without roads leading up to it: the roads have since disappeared or were never built.

The steel supporting structure of these two bridges has a tree-like character, inspired by the surrounding forest. The innovative design of the large steel road bridge was preferred by the client thanks to the fact that the design was more attractive but cost the same compared to a typical concrete design. After it had been built, the relevant authorities were so pleased with the design that a pedestrian bridge with a similar structure was added in 2008, completing the Traunstein bridge ensemble. The tree-frame supporting structure of both bridges uses comparatively little steel thanks to the optimal load support. The deck of the road bridge is slim concrete composite slab: for the pedestrian bridge the deck and roof comprise a filigree timber construction.

TRAUNSTEIN BRIDGE ENSEMBLE
TRAUNSTEIN, GERMANY

Architect: Richard J. Dietrich Büro für Ingenieur-Architektur
Structural engineers: Köppl Ingenieure
Location: over the Traun, Traunstein, Germany
Length: 214.5 m and 46 m
Completion: 2000 and 2008
Client: Municipality of Traunstein
Bridge type: truss bridge

"Praise the bridge that carried you over." –
George Colman, English writer

The design of this bridge should be understood as a modern interpretation of the historical arch bridge, although it in no way attempts to copy it. It is modest in form, only the section crossing the river is emphasized by the arches over the bridge deck. The construction takes second place to the surrounding landscape, but is nevertheless an exciting architectural element thanks to its almost sculptural character. The carefully selected slim construction solution has a minimal impact on the riverbanks. An optical tension is created by the correspondence between arches and V-shaped supports. The V-shaped supports transition smoothly into the arches, thus connecting the foreshore bridges with the section crossing the river and providing all elements with a formal unity.

WALD-SCHLÖSSCHEN-BRÜCKE
DRESDEN, GERMANY

Architects: Kolb Ripke Architekten
Structural engineers: Eisenloffel + Sattler Ingenieure, Meyer + Schubart Ingenieure, VIC Brücken- und Ingenieurbau
Length: 636 m
Completion: 2013
Client: Straßen- und Tiefbauamt der Landeshauptstadt Dresden
Bridge type: arched bridge

"The wisdom of bridges comes from the fact that they know the both sides, they know the both shores!" – Mehmet Murat Ildan, Turkish author

The original covered wooden bridge was swept away by floodwater and debris at the end of August, 2005. A new wooden bridge was designed as a replacement; the primary construction comprises a 45-meter-long timber frame of glued laminated timber. The lower chords have a steel profile of HEB 360, and are attached to the diagonal rods with slotted metal panels. The upper chords are also attached with slotted connections. The bridge deck comprises water resistant wooden panels and is arranged so that the panels run across rather than along the deck and are screwed to the wooden frame.

ENNIGER BRIDGE
MALTERS, SWITZERLAND

Architects: Pirmin Jung Ingenieure für Holzbau
Structural engineers: Pirmin Jung Ingenieure für Holzbau
Location: Kleine Emme, 6102 Malters, Switzerland
Length: 43 m
Completion: 2010
Client: Strassengenossenschaft Ennigerbrücke
Bridge type: lattice bridge

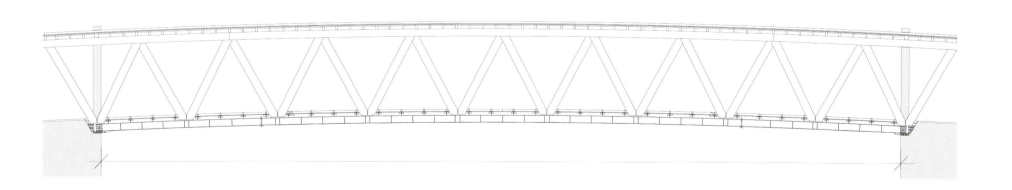

"I like to build bridges... not walls." —
Oscar Arias Sanchez, Costa Rican president

BRIDGE SCHOOL
XIASHI, CHINA

The Bridge School bridges the two parts of the small village of Xiashi that lie on either side of a small creek running about ten meters below the village. The structure is created by two steel trusses that span the creek with the space between them housing the functions of the school. Suspended from the structure and running below it is a pedestrian bridge for the people of the village to use. The school has become the physical and spiritual center of what was a declining village. Placed in such a way that it addresses its surroundings, the Bridge School connects two villages together, providing a central, social space. The result is a project that has successfully invigorated the entire community, encapsulating social sustainability through architectural intervention.

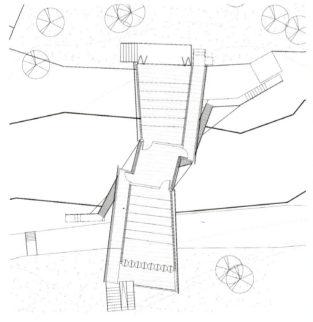

Architects: Li Xiaodong/atelier
Location: Xiashi village, Pinghe county, Fujian province, China
Surface: 240 m²
Completion: 2009
Client: Xiashi village
Bridge type: cantilever and girder bridge

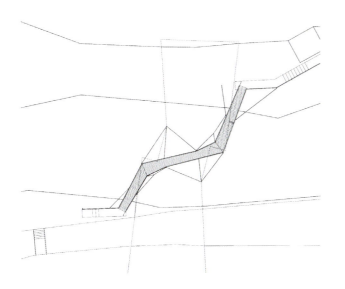

A bridge built in Lima, Peru, in 1610 was made of mortar that was mixed not with water but with the whites of 10,000 eggs. The bridge, appropriately called the Bridge of Eggs, is still standing.

Architects: Next architects
Structural engineers: ABT Adviesbureau voor Bouwtechniek
Location: Carnisselande, Barendrecht, The Netherlands
Length: 96 m
Completion: 2013
Client: Municipality of Barendrecht
Bridge type: folly

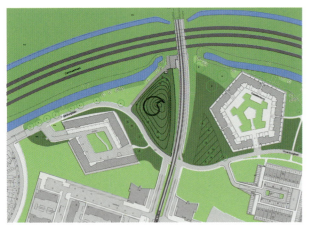

ELASTIC PERSPECTIVE
BARENDRECHT, THE NETHERLANDS

This design comprises a circular stair that leads visitors up to a height that allows an unhindered view of the horizon. The path is arranged in one continuous movement and therefore plays on the context of the heavy infrastructural surroundings of ring road and tram track. Based on the principal of the Möbius strip, the continuous route of the stair is a delusion; it has only one surface and can only exist as a three-dimensional object. Upside becomes underside, becomes upside. Because of its structure, the shape of the object is hard to perceive; every perspective generates a new image with which the design is not only a contextual but also a very literal answer to the given context of the local art plan: an Elastic Perspective.

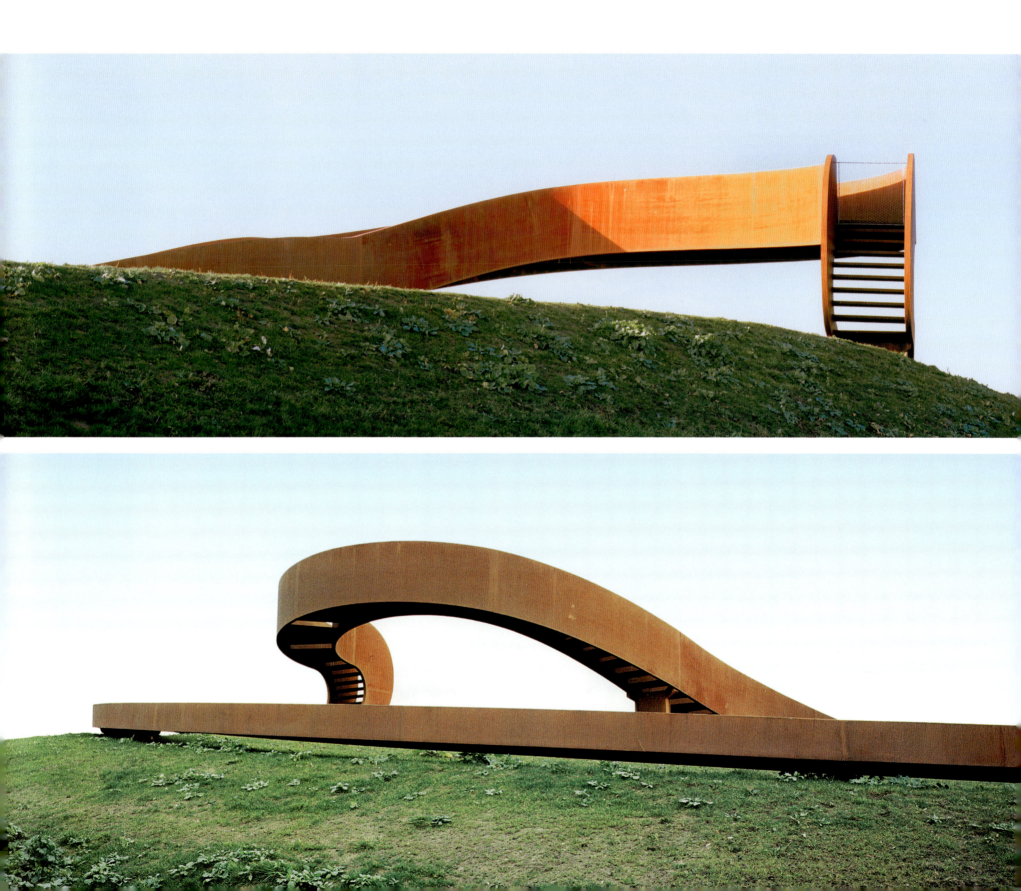

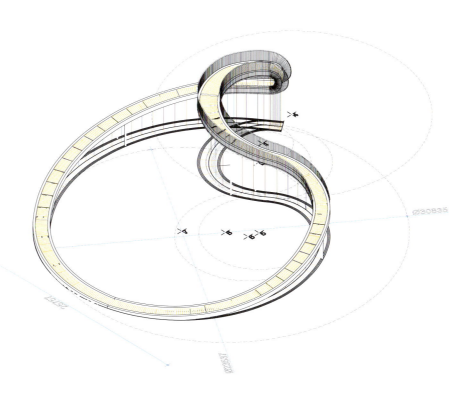

106 << 107

"A bridge enables us to experience our daily environment from another perspective" – Michel Schreinemachers, Dutch architect

The new Kirchenbrücke is made of Muotathal spruce wood and was largely built by people from the local area. Connecting the two separate parts of the village, the bridge spans over the turbulent Muota river and has a length of approximately 33 meters. The bridge was built to replace the original Trogbrücke, which was located slightly further downstream, and offers motorists and pedestrians more space and improved safety. The bridge deck almost appears to float below the suspended arched girders, hanging from steel tension rods. The bridge deck has two lanes for traffic and can bear loads of up to 40 tons. The footpath offers a safe way for pedestrians and cyclists to cross the river.

KIRCHENBRÜCKE
MUOTATHAL, GERMANY

Architects: Eduard Imhof, Architekt
Structural engineers: Pirmin Jung Ingenieure für Holzbau
Length: 33 m
Completion: 2009
Client: Gemeinde Muotathal
Bridge type: arched bridge

"Many a calm river begins as a turbulent waterfall, yet none hurtles and foams all the way to the sea." – Mikhail Lermontov, Russian author

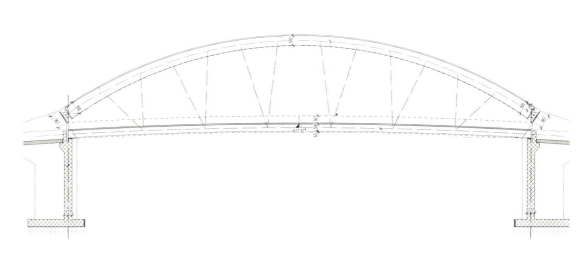

This project involved replacing an existing highway bridge with two wider bridges. A filigree supporting steel structure was used to counter the rather dominating appearance of the bridge in the landscape, comprising two steel tube trusses with a light deck made of reinforced concrete composite. The rhythm of the bridge structure follows the shape of the valley. The concrete pillars are round and narrow; their arrangement interrupts views as little as possible. A six-meter noise protection barrier is also integrated into the design. The construction of the bridge is to be carried out in phases and many of the parts used are prefabricated. This saves a considerable amount of building time.

HIGHWAY BRIDGE
WÜRZBURG, GERMANY

Architect: Richard J. Dietrich Büro für Ingenieur-Architektur
Structural engineers: Krebs und Kiefer Ingenieure GmbH
Location: Highway BAB A3 Würzburg-Nuremberg, Germany
Length: 660 m
Completion: ongoing
Client: Autobahndirektion Nordbayern
Bridge type: steel spaceframe bridge

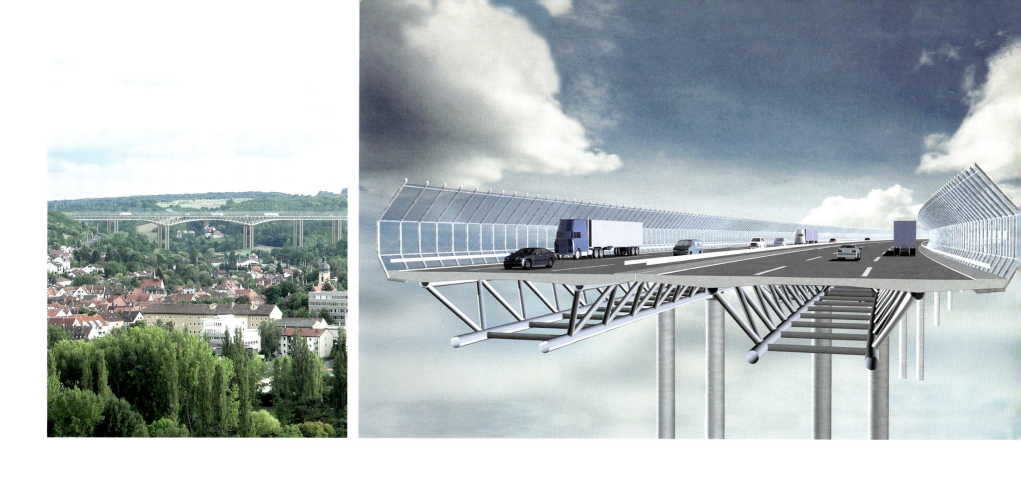

The name of the card game "Bridge" stems from the Russian word "Biritsch", which means "herald".

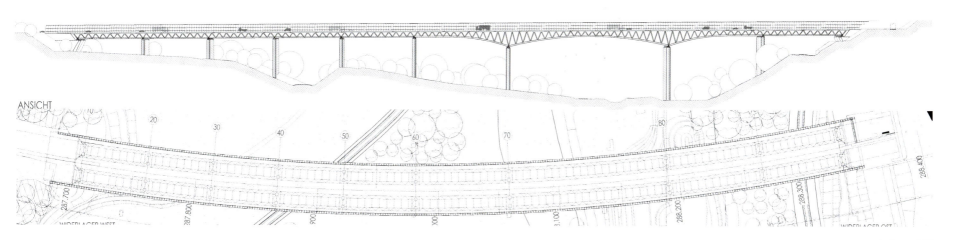

PHYLLIS J. TILLEY MEMORIAL FOOTBRIDGE
FORT WORTH, TX, USA

The Phyllis J. Tilley Memorial Footbridge is innovative, elegant and sustainable. The first arch-supported stress ribbon bridge in the US spans the Trinity River close to downtown, connecting the central business area with the city's Cultural District, beckoning pedestrians and bicyclists to use the City's extensive trail system along the waterfront. An unconventional structural bridge combination was selected to address the site conditions, visual objectives and the desire of the city to build a special and memorable footbridge along the river. This bridge has become a visual asset along the river and a new symbol of the city.

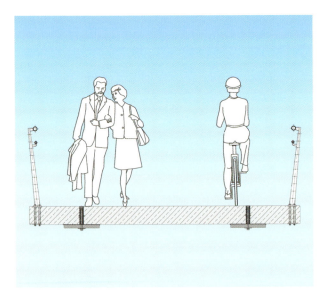

Architects: Rosales + Partners
Structural engineers: Freese and Nichols, Inc.,
Schlaich Bergermann and Partner, LP
Location: crosses the Trinity River in Fort Worth, TX, USA
Length: 112 m
Completion: 2012
Client: City of Fort Worth, Texas
Bridge type: arched bridge

Four of the five longest bridges in the world are part of the Beijing-Shanghai High-Speed Railway, the other is part of the Xuzhou-Lanzhou High-Speed Railway.

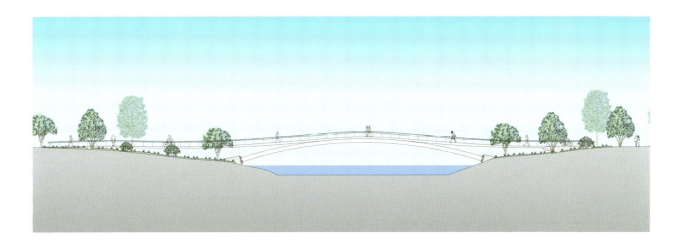

Architects: West 8 urban design & landscape architecture
Structural engineers: BAS – Dirk Jaspaert
Location: Station Aarschot, 3200 Aarschot, Belgium
Length: 105 m
Completion: 2011
Client: City of Aarschot, Infrabel en de NMBS Holding
Bridge type: truss bridge

AARSCHOT PEDES-TRIAN BRIDGE
AARSCHOT, BELGIUM

West 8's design for a new bridge across rail tracks near Aarschot, focuses on the functional character of the bridge as well as on its potential to seduce and surprise the visitor. The bridge is an important link in the regional bicycle network. A monolithic natural stone pedestal separates the rails and the square. The spacing of the station platforms and heavy goods tracks below allow for the placement of multiple columns and for the construction of a bridge with several relatively short spans. The bridge design relates strongly to the 'industrial' atmosphere of station, engines, cargo transport and steel rail tracks.

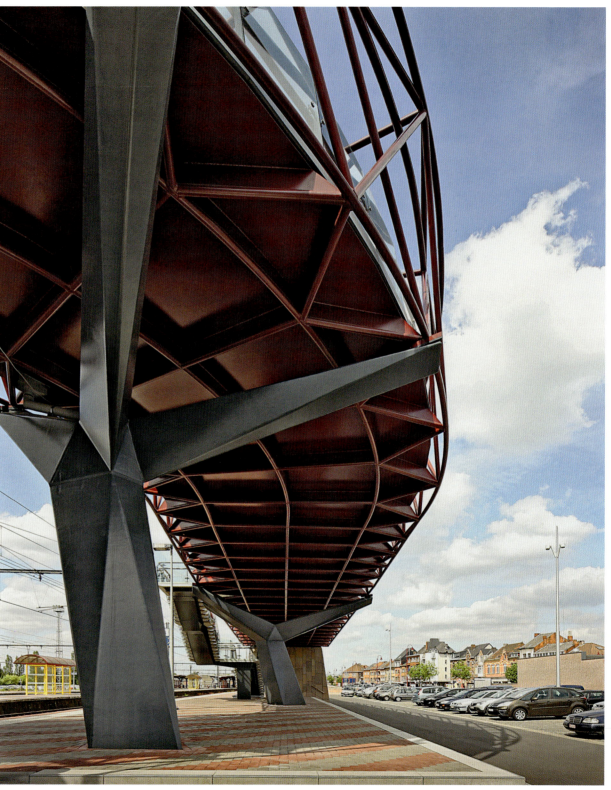

"The Golden Gate Bridge is one of the greatest monuments of all time. ... What has been thus played up in form should not be let down in color." —
Irving Morrow, American architect

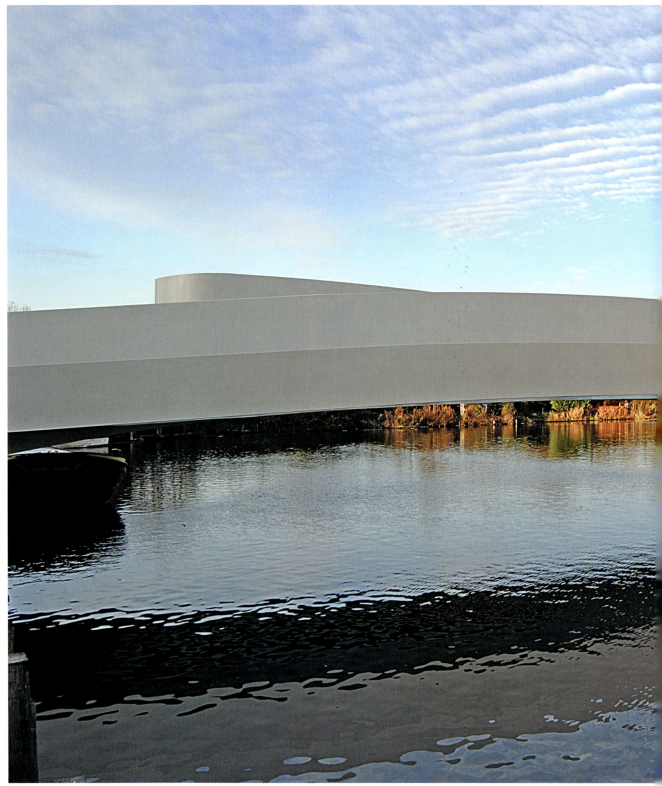

The Olympic Stadium Bridge is part of the new public space around the Olympic stadium in the north-west area of Amsterdam-Zuid. The 1928 Olympic stadium was completely renovated and updated to meet contemporary standards in the late 1990s. The bridge provides access to the public space on the north-west side of the stadium. On the other side of the water, it connects to a roundabout which guides traffic to the Aldo van Eijck's Burgerweeshuis. In terms of its design and materiality, the bridge has an autonomous identity which is not related to the completely different worlds on both sides of the water. Two viewpoints are designed on a corner positioned at the level of the bank. At this point the bridge is connected with the water via an opening in the bridge-deck.

NA DRUK GELUKBRUG
AMSTERDAM, THE NETHERLANDS

Architects: René van Zuuk Architects
Structural engineers: ABT bv
Location: Olympic Stadium, Amsterdam, The Netherlands
Length: 80 m
Completion: 2013
Client: Municipality of Amsterdam
Bridge type: arched bridge

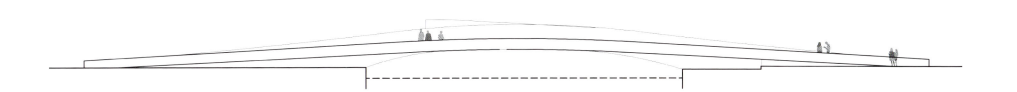

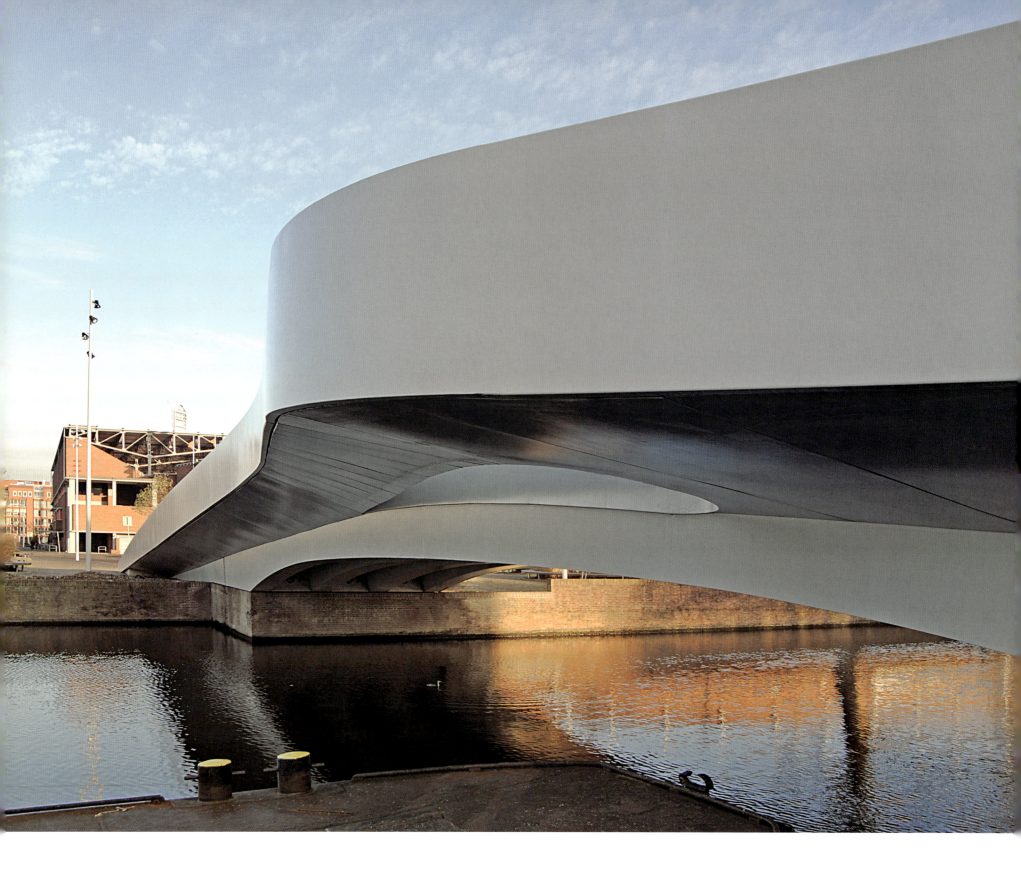

The Sydney Harbour Bridge was opened by Jack Lang in 1932. As he was about to cut the ribbon, a man rode up on a horse, slashed the ribbon with his sword and opened the bridge in the name of the people of New South Wales. He was promptly arrested.

Architects: nooyoon by Hyuntek Yoon
Location: Ozone Park, New York, NY, USA
Length: 175 m
Client: Emerging New York Architects Committee, AIA New York Chapter
Bridge type: reverse arched bridge

UPSIDE DOWN BRIDGE
NEW YORK CITY, NY, USA

The Queensway is one of New York's abandoned railways, located in Queens. The Queensway once represented connection and productivity, but now it is just an example of leftover urban infrastructure. The Upside Down Bridge project proposes an overturned bridge be used to connect the ground with the vertically isolated space above. The Upside Down Bridge opens up the visual and physical corridors between two urban fabrics and creates a smooth transition from the ground to the railway. The intersection between this vertical and horizontal connection, called The Plaza, will be used as a versatile public space. Upside Down Bridge will be reproduced at several locations from the southern section to the northern section of the railway to help activate local communities.

Venice has 426 bridges, Amsterdam 1,539 and Hamburg 2,496. But New York City wins with a grand total of 2,891 bridges.

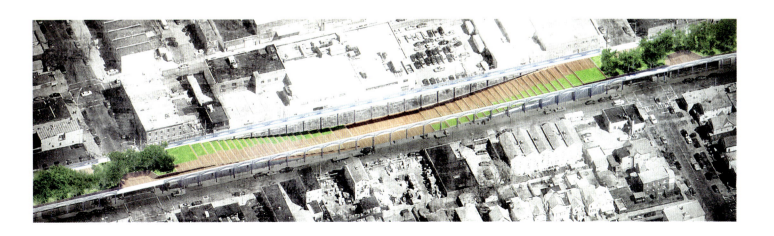

This new bridge over the Stör near Itzehoe will replace the existing bridge on the A23 highway. The supporting pillars are made of concrete, while the supporting structure beneath the road is made of steel. The roads in both directions are built as independent bridges. The pillars of the foreshore bridges are conceived as "steppers", which are wider at the bottom than the top, almost giving the impression that the bridge is striding forwards. The pillars supporting the section of the bridge that spans the river stretch across the width on both riverbanks, giving the bridge an appearance reminiscent of a viaduct. The arches over the river have a height of around 23 meters and a length of 120 meters.

STÖRBRÜCKE
ITZEHOE, GERMANY

Architects: Winking · Froh Architekten
Structural engineers: Ingenieurbüro Grassl
Length: 120 m
Completion: 2014
Client: Landesbetrieb Straßenbau und Verkehr Schleswig-Holstein
Bridge type: arched bridge

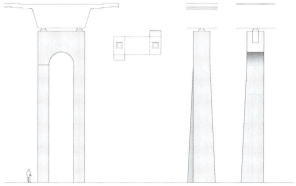

PEACE BRIDGE
CALGARY, CANADA

The Peace Bridge is a landmark structure connecting the north side of the river, which is richly landscaped with trees and grassed slopes, with the south side, a modern urban landscape. The structured shape is defined by a helix developed over an oval cross section with two clearly defined tangential radii creating an architectural space within. The upper openings are filled with glazed leaves bent to the same shape as the exterior of the helical form offering protection to the users from the rain and winter weather conditions. Light elements below the deck pick out the sculptural appearance of the underside of the bridge at night, creating graceful reflections of the bridge in the water below.

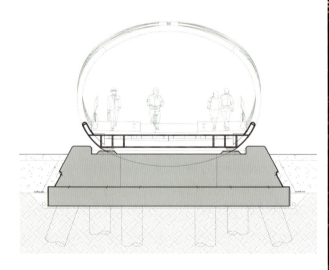

Architects: Santiago Calatrava
Structural engineers: Santiago Calatrava
Location: Sunnyside/Eau Claire Park, Calgary, Canada
Length: 126 m
Completion: 2012
Client: City of Calgary
Bridge type: helical-formed steel bridge

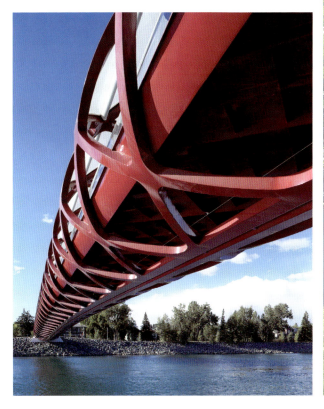

"We must combine the urban landscape with nature. Bridges are a perfect means to do so because they cross waterways that bring a flow of nature into the cityscape." – Santiago Calatrava, Spanish architect, engineer, artist

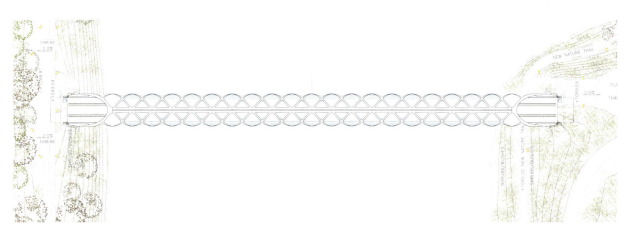

HELIX BRIDGE
SINGAPORE, SINGAPORE

The Helix Bridge is named after its structure. In addition to its uniqueness of structure and form, it was designed to respond to its particular setting at the opening of the Singapore River to Marina Bay. The concept derived initially from the desire to curve the plan of the bridge so that it sweeps down onto promenades either side. Having selected the design in an international design competition, Singapore's Urban Redevelopment Authority decided that it should be constructed entirely in stainless steel. This decision enabled the tubes, struts and ties to be finely crafted, the multiple connection joints being designed to appear organic. These details, and the helix form overall, led to the bridge being popularly compared to the DNA molecule, with its connotations of 'life-giving' and 'sustainability'.

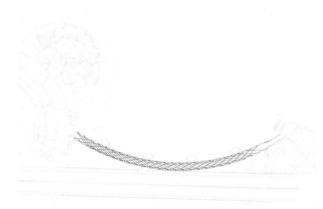

Architects: Cox Architecture, Architects 61
Structural engineers: Arup
Location: Raffles Avenue and Bayfront Bridge, Singapore, Singapore
Length: 280 m
Completion: 2010
Client: Municipality of Singapore
Bridge type: truss bridge

"You only make a bridge where there is a river" –
African proverb

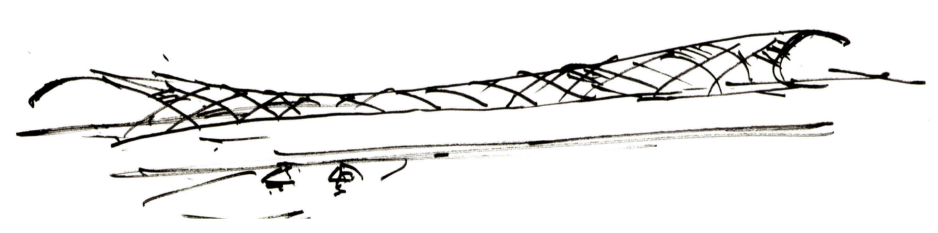

BRIDGE OF STRINGS
JERUSALEM, ISRAEL

At the request of the City of Jerusalem, Santiago Calatrava designed a new bridge in the city's key area near the Central Bus Station as a part of the Jerusalem Light Rail mass transit system. The light rail bridge rises over a busy traffic intersection, curving in an S-form as it extends from Jaffa Street to Herzl Boulevard. To accommodate this difficult location, Calatrava designed a cable-stayed bridge, with the cables anchored to a single sloping pylon sited at the center of the "S". The pylon is exceptionally light and slender, drawing attention to the cables that resemble the strings of a harp. A public plaza was created under the bridge and the bridge itself serves as a new gateway to the city.

Architects: Santiago Calatrava
Structural engineers: Santiago Calatrava
Location: Jaffa Street/Herzl Boulevard, Jerusalem, Israel
Length: 360 m
Completion: 2008
Client: Moriah Jerusalem Development Co. Ltd.
Bridge type: cable-stayed bridge

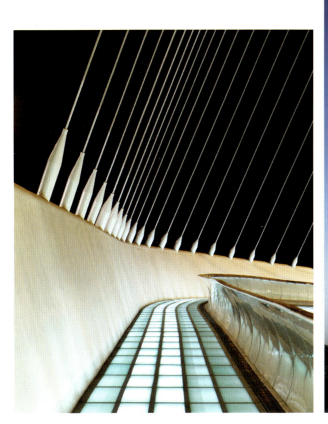

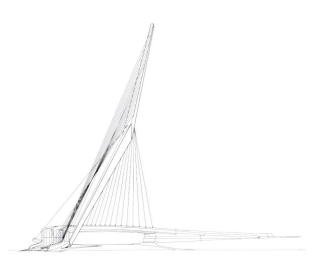

"We build too many walls and not enough bridges." – Isaac Newton, English physicist and mathematician

The seele glass bridge constitutes the world's first prototype of a bridge made of cold-bent glass. The bridge comprises just three structural glass components: a floor glass panel that is curved in elevation, and two glass balustrades that curve inwards in plan. The glass arch and balustrades are connected through a load-bearing silicone adhesive joint. The use of cold-bent glass panels, a complex spatial and stiffness-dependent structural behaviour and the extensive use of load-bearing adhesive joints are the characteristic features of the glass bridge. This exceptional transparent experiment ventures on the threshold of designing structural glass components and represents a prototype for future structural glass applications.

SEELE GLASS BRIDGE
DÜSSELDORF, GERMANY

Architects: IBK Forschung + Entwicklung
Structural engineers: Engelsmann Peters Beratende Ingenieure
Development and realization: sedak GmbH & Co. KG
Location: glasstec 2008 Düsseldorf, Germany
Length: 7 m
Completion: 2008
Client: sedak GmbH & Co. KG
Bridge type: girder bridge

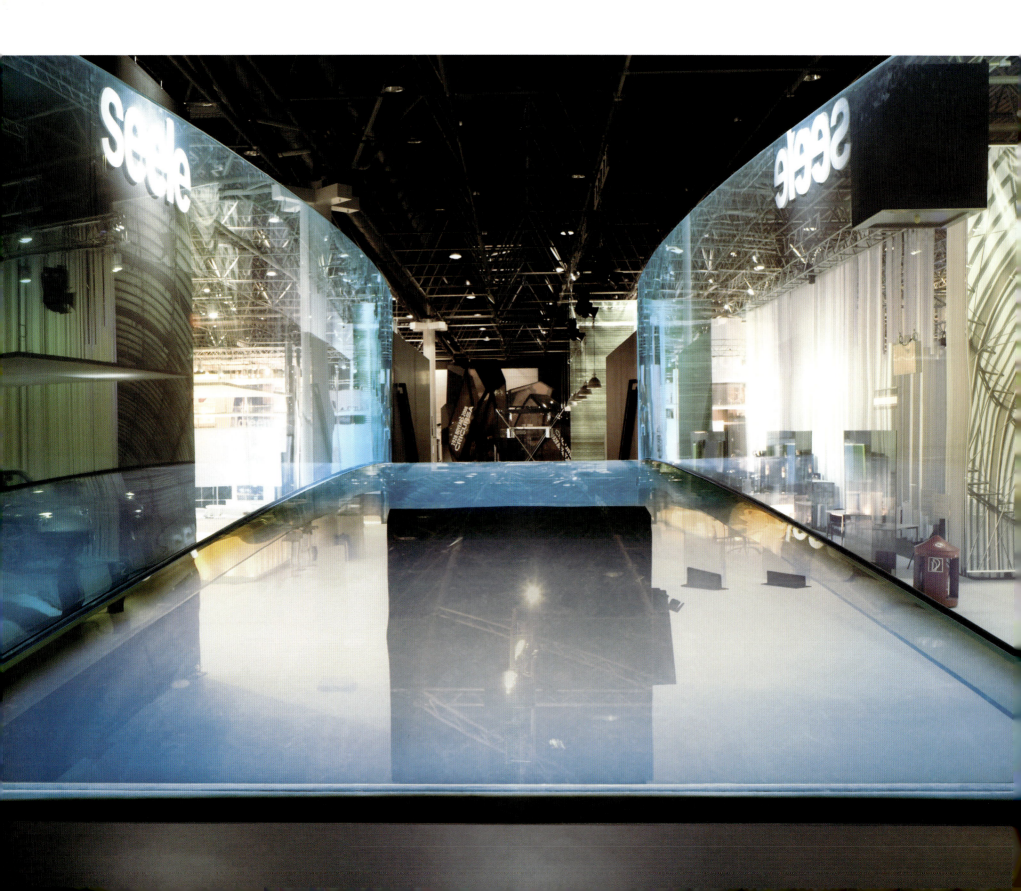

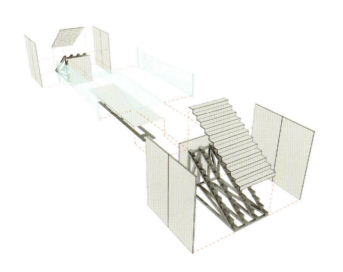

"A great bridge is a great monument which should serve to make known the splendour and genius of a nation." – Jean Peronnet, French engineer

Architects: MLRP Architecture, research and development
Structural engineers: Grontmij
Location: Fælledparken, Copenhagen, Denmark
Length: 35 m
Completion: 2012
Client: City of Copenhagen, McKinney-Møller's Fund
Bridge type: arched bridge

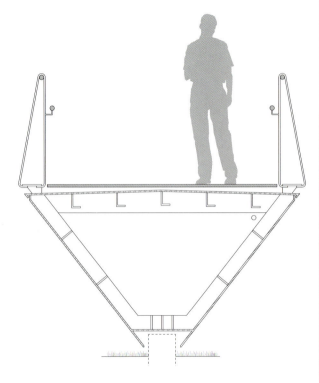

WOVEN BRIDGE
COPENHAGEN, DENMARK

The Woven Bridge is a modern interpretation of a classical steel park footbridge, allowing new perspectives of the park and lake. The bridge is located at the southern end of the lake and creates a new shortcut when crossing through the park. The foundations are concealed under the steel structure making the transition between bridge and nature more natural. The bridge gets its name from its steel railing, made of bent steel bars, which resemble a continuous woven thread. The railing gives the bridge a unique character and together with the slim structure, makes the bridge more of a design object than a practicality. The steel used for the railing has been galvanized and painted before mounting.

The Overseas Highway includes 42 bridges that connect the islands of the Florida Keys.

GREEN SCHOOL MILLENIUM BRIDGE
BALI, INDONESIA

The Green School Millennium Bridge has become an important icon for the Green School and for bamboo architecture worldwide. Located in Sibang Kaja, Bali, it traverses the Ayung River to connect the east and west areas of the Green School campus. The bridge span is twenty-two meters, and all the structural elements are made of bamboo except for the foundations and connection points. It uses 5,000 meters of bamboo materials and took four months to construct. The roof shape is inspired by the local architectural style of the Minangkabau people. This bridge is an example of the limitless possibilities when architects, engineers, and bamboo craftsmen collaborate to create new paradigms in architecture.

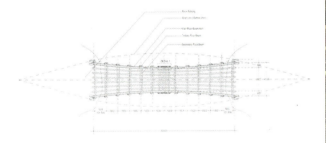

Architects: Ibuku
Structural engineers: Ashar Saputra, Ketut Sudarsara
Location: Jalan Raya Sibang Kaja, Banjar Saren, Badung, Bali, Indonesia
Length: 22 m
Completion: 2011
Client: Green School
Bridge type: arched bridge

"Architecture is a bridge between the earth and the air." – Renzo Piano, Italian architect

Responding to the current pinch-points where the streetscape meets the water's edge, these new public space gateways have been created in some of the most heavily used parts of the Toronto waterfront. The geometry of each deck is carefully conceived using playful curves that are constantly changing to create ledges for seating and new routes to access the water's edge. The configuration of stairs act as an informal amphitheater and the varying heights of the deck ultimately allow for different experiences of both the lake and the city. The timber beams that span the width of the slips also form the stairs, risers, and treads of the deck. The first three completed WaveDecks provide a dramatic beginning to Toronto's planned waterfront revitalization.

WAVEDECKS
TORONTO, CANADA

Architects: West 8 urban design & landscape architecture
Structural engineers: West 8 urban design & landscape architecture
Location: 1 Rees St, Toronto, M5V 3A7, Canada
Length: 3,500 m
Completion: 2009
Client: Waterfront Toronto
Bridge type: curving bridge

The song "Bridge over Troubled Water" (1970) was the titlesong of the last studio album by Simon & Garfunkel, who split up the same year.

Suspended from three large helium balloons, this bridge is an interesting twist on traditional suspension bridges. Designed by French artist Olivier Grossetête, the bridge was an art exhibition displayed at the Tatton Park Biennial in England in 2012. Located in the park's Japanese Garden, the bridge is made of cedar and held together by ropes. Although the bridge is not functional, it would theoretically hold the weight of one person. The artist says that the work is intended to bring life to dreams and poetry in everyday life.

MONKEY BRIDGE
TATTON, UNITED KNIGDOM

Designer: Olivier Grossetête
Location: Tatton Park Biennial, Tatton, United Kingdom
Length: 22 m
Completion: 2012
Client: Tatton Park Biennial
Bridge type: suspension bridge suspended from helium balloons

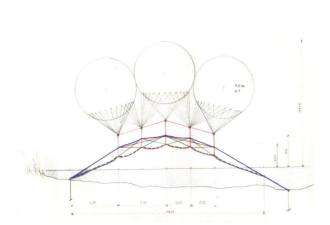

"Don't cross the bridge till you come to it." –
English proverb

Bouncing Bridge is an inflatable bridge equipped with giant trampolines, dedicated to the joyful release from gravity as one bounces above the river. Its intended location is near the Bir-Hakeim Bridge and the design uses inflatable modules 30 meters in diameter. A trampoline mesh is stretched across the central part of each ring. The floating buoys are attached together by cord to form a stable and self-supporting ensemble. The total length of the bridge is approximately 94 meters. Bouncing Bridge allows every visitor a novel view of Paris from his or her own unique spatial position. The close proximity of this project to the Eiffel Tower reveals a specific kind of architecture: one designed to install an experience of happiness in the city.

BOUNCING BRIDGE
PARIS, FRANCE

Architects: AZC
Structural engineers: TP Arquitectura i Construcció Tèxtil
Surface: 2,100 m²
Client: ArchTriumph
Bridge type: inflatable floating bridge

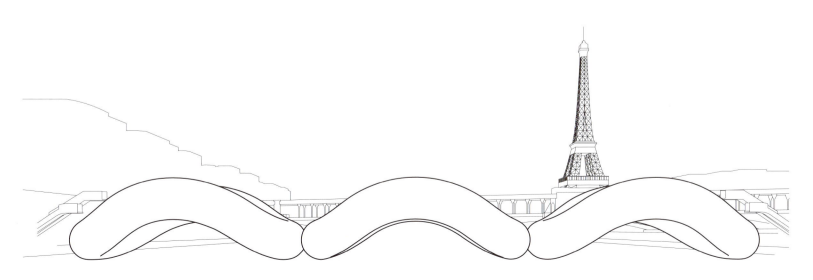

The Governor Albert D. Rosellini Bridge at Evergreen Point, Seattle, WA, is the longest floating bridge in the world: it is 2,310 meters long.

MELKWEGBRIDGE
PURMEREND, THE NETHERLANDS

The Melkwegbridge is the key project in the De Kanaalsprong master plan and connects the historic city center with the new urban expansion. The most striking part of the bridge is a massive arch that offers an incredible view over the city. The high lookout is an attraction in itself and lets pedestrians fully experience the connection between the new and historic centers of Purmerend. Bicycles cross the bridge using the 100-meter-long bicycle deck, designed as a pendulum over the water. Both bridge sections connect fluently together. This unity is enhanced by the continuity of materials and colors. LED lights follow the contours of the bridge and guarantee a spectacular view even after sunset.

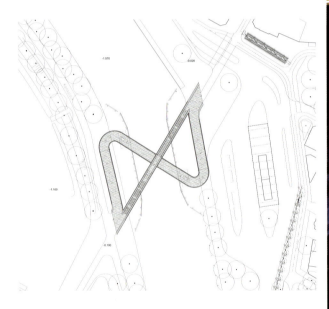

Architects: Next architects
Structural engineers: Ingenieurs Bureau Amsterdam (IBA),
ABT Adviesbureau voor Bouwtechniek
Location: Melkweg, Purmerend, The Netherlands
Length: 66 m
Completion: 2012
Client: Municipality of Purmerend
Bridge type: moveable bridge

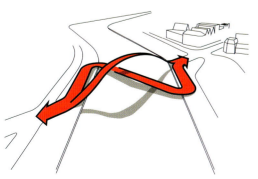

"A bridge is more than only a connection from A to B, it becomes a destination in itself." – Marijn Schenk, Dutch architect

ELB BRIDGE
U-BAHN STATION
HAMBURG, GERMANY

Architects von Gerkan, Marg und Partner (gmp) won first prize in a competition to design the Elb Bridge U-Bahn station. The genius loci of this station is determined by its location direct on the Elbe and the historical Elb Bridge with its sweeping steel arches. A suspended glass curtain offers protection from the weather. The light-flooded station provides interesting views of the new quarter on Baaken Harbor, the skyscrapers and the other Elb bridges. The design is characterized by its clear and simple structure. A light and media installation is envisaged between the platform and the ticket hall. The lighting design is modest and modern, underlining the character of the building.

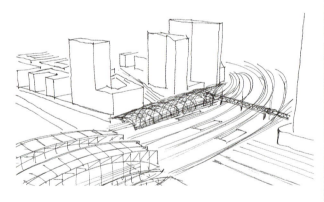

Architects: gmp Architekten von Gerkan, Marg und Partner
Structural engineers: schlaich bergermann und partner
Location: Hamburg-Elbbrücken, HafenCity, Hamburg, Germany
Length: 40 m
Completion: ongoing
Client: Hamburger Hochbahn
Bridge type: truss bridge

The bridge with the longest span in the world (distance between two supporting pillars) is the Akashi-Kaikyō-Bridge in Japan, which was built in 1998 and boasts a distance of 1990.8 meters.

MAX-GLEISSNER-BRÜCKE
TIRSCHENREUTH, GERMANY

Built within the framework of the regional horticultural show 2013 "Natur in Tirschenreuth", this stress-ribbon bridge creates an urban connection that serves as a pedestrian and cycle bridge. Just two bands of 25-millimeter-thick steel support the entire bridge deck. Thus, the view across the pond under the bridge is not interrupted by supporting columns or pillars. The timber 'body' of the bridge is intended as reminder of the importance of wood in the history of the town of Tirschenreuth and also shares a direct dialogue with the regional architecture. The stress-ribbon bridge has a length of 85 meters. Two abutments are situated on each bank; the visible parts of these are built of high quality concrete.

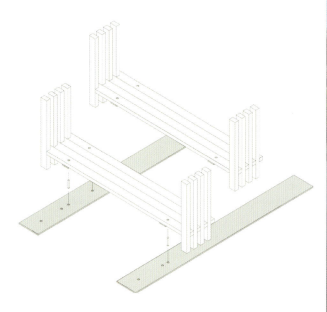

Architects: Annabau Architektur und Landschaft, Moritz Schloten
Structural engineers: Schüssler-Plan Ingenieurgesellschaft, Wolfgang Strobl
Location: 95643 Tirschenreuth, Germany
Length: 85 m
Completion: 2013
Client: Municipality of Tirschenreuth
Bridge type: stress-ribbon bridge

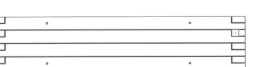

"But some day our questions will be answers and we'll be caught in something so bright…and every step I take is one step closer on a bridge we must cross to meet." – Richard Bach, American writer

Architects: ONL [Oosterhuis_Lénárd]
Structural engineers: Lukassen Brokking
Location: intersection between Nico Bolkensteinlaan and N348,
the Netherlands
Length: 150 m
Completion: 2011
Client: Municipality of Deventer
Bridge type: cantilever and girder bridge

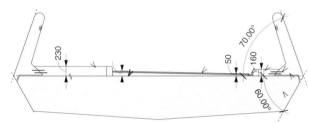

D-SPLINE
DEVENTER, THE NETHERLANDS

The D-Spline is a bridge for pedestrians and cyclists, spanning a road and the Overijssel canal in Deventer. ONL's design endeavors to capture the essence of the span with one fluid motion. One long slightly crowned elastic line determines the contour of the bridge. All remaining lines do their part to enhance the impression of fluid motion, giving the bridge its slender sculptural character. The 150-meter-long surface just above the crease line reflects the sky irrespective of weather conditions. ONL has chosen to build the bridge out of a single material to attain a monolithic architectural appearance.

"The strongest bridges are built from the stones of fallen walls." – Andreas Tenzer, German philosopher

The high-speed rail bridge lies along the railway route from Erfurt to Leipzig/Halle. The construction gave the bridge an unusually transparent, slim and elegant appearance, thus impacting as little as possible on the rural surroundings. The superstructure is connected to the west abutment by eleven massive reinforced concrete pillars. The length of the bridge presented the engineers with a challenge. Until now, bridges of this length have not been built as integral constructions. With this bridge, the DB AG continues the historical tradition of railway viaducts, implementing an innovative bridge design. Ludolf Krontal (today Marx Krontal, Hanover) and Stephan Sonnabend (Büchting + Streit, Munich) received the German Bridge Construction Prize in 2012.

SCHERKONDETAL-BRÜCKE
KRAUTHEIM, GERMANY

Structural engineers: DB ProjektBau, Ludolf Krontal, (today Ingenieurbüro Marx Krontal), Büchting + Streit, Stephan Sonnabend
Location: Weimarer Land near Krautheim, Germany
Completion: 2011
Client: DB Netz
Length: 577 m
Bridge type: semi-integral pre-stressed concrete bridge

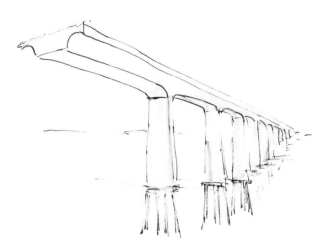

The French song "Sur le Pont d'Avignon" was originally played as "Sous le pont"; so not on, but rather under the bridge. It was only when it had been forgotten that the city's entertainment quarter was once located on the island under the bridge that the text changed.

INDEX

ABT ADVIESBUREAU VOOR BOUWTECHNIEK
www.abt.eu — 104, 128, 180

ANNABAU ARCHITEKTUR UND LANDSCHAFT,
MORITZ SCHLOTEN
www.annabau.com — 190

ARCHITECTS 61
www.a61.com.sg — 146

Arup
www.arup.com — 146

COX ARCHITECTURE
www.coxarchitecture.com.au — 146

ERCAN AĞIRBAŞ FRIENDS
www.eafriends.eu — 34

DIETMAR FEICHTINGER ARCHITECTES
www.feichtingerarchitectes.com — 82

FOSTER + PARTNERS
www.fosterandpartners.com — 56

FREESE AND NICHOLS, INC.
www.freese.com — 118

FUTURE CITIES LAB,
NATALY GATTEGNO + JASON KELLY JOHNSON
www.future-cities-lab.net — 52

GMP ARCHITEKTEN VON GERKAN, MARG UND PARTNER
www.gmp-architekten.de — 186

INGENIEURBÜRO GRASSL
www.grassl-ing.de — 138

GRONTMIJ
www.grontmij.dk — 44, 158

OLIVIER GROSSETÊTE — 170

GRUNER + WEPF INGENIEURE
www.grunerwepf.ch — 64

FERDINAND HEIDE ARCHITEKT
www.ferdinand-heide.de — 44

IBK FORSCHUNG + ENTWICKLUNG — 154

IBUKU
www.ibuku.com — 162

EDUARD IMHOF, ARCHITEKT — 110

INGENIEURS BUREAU AMSTERDAM (IBA)
www.iba.amsterdam.nl — 180

IPV DELFT
www.ipvdelft.com — 72

ERHARD KARGEL
www.kargel.co.at — 14, 28

KOLB RIPKE ARCHITEKTEN
www.kolbripke.de — 60, 78, 90

KÖPPL INGENIEURE
www.koeppl-ingenieure.de — 86

KREBS UND KIEFER INGENIEURE GMBH
www.kuk.de — 114

MARX KRONTAL
www.marxkrontal.com — 202

LEUPPI & SCHAFROTH ARCHITEKTEN
www.leuppischafroth.ch — 64

BIURO PROJEKTÓW LEWICKI ŁATAK
www.lewicki-latak.com.pl — 40

LUKASSEN BROKKING
www.lukassenbrokking.nl — 196

MEYER + SCHUBART INGENIEURE
www.meyer-schubart.de — 90

MLRP ARCHITECTURE, RESEARCH AND DEVELOPMENT
www.mlrp.dk — 158

MOSTY WROCŁAW			SCHÜSSLER-PLAN INGENIEURGESELLSCHAFT	
www.mosty-wroclaw.com.pl	40		www.schuessler-plan.de	34, 190
NEXT ARCHITECTS			TP Arquitectura i Construcció Tèxtil	174
www.nextarchitects.com	104, 180			
			VIC– BRÜCKEN UND INGENIEURBAU	
NOOYOON BY HYUNTEK YOON			www.vic-gmbh.de	78, 90
www.nooyoon.com	134			
			HANS WAGNER/ABES	
OMA			www.abes.at	14, 28
www.oma.eu	68			
			WEST 8 URBAN DESIGN & LANDSCAPE ARCHITECTURE	
ONL [OOSTERHUIS_LÉNÁRD]			www.west8.com	24, 124, 166
www.oosterhuis.nl	196			
			BRUCE WILLIAMS	
PIRMIN JUNG INGENIEURE FÜR HOLZBAU			www.brucewilliams.net	48
www.pirminjung.ch	94, 110			
			WINKING · FROH ARCHITEKTEN	
RENÉ VAN ZUUK ARCHITECTS			www.winking-froh.de	138
www.renevanzuuk.nl	128			
			WITTEVEEN+BOS	
RFR			www.witteveenbos.nl	72
www.rfr-group.com	82			
			WSP	
ROSALES + PARTNERS			www.wspgroup.com	68
www.rosalespartners.com	118			
			LI XIAODONG/ATELIER	
ASHAR SAPUTRA, KETUT SUDARSARA	162		www.lixiaodong.net	100
			WIENSTROER ARCHITEKTEN STADTPLANER	
SCHLAICH BERGERMANN UND PARTNER			www.wienstroer-architekten.de	34
www.sbp.de	186			

PICTURE CREDITS

AirStudio, Orléans 175–177 r., 178 · David Boureau 82–84 · CEVM / Foster + Partners / D. Jamme 56–59 a. · R. J. Dietrich, Martina Brosig 114–117 · Filip Dujardin 124–127 · EG Focus / Wikimedia Commons 6 · Foster + Partners 59 b. · Greg Folkins 120–122, 123 a. l. · free2rec/Ignacio Linares 60–63, 78–81, 90 · Gärtner & Christ 186–189 · Ingenieurbüro Grassl 139 · Sergio Grazia, Paris 174, 177 l., 179 · Frank Heinen, Michael Wolff 44–47 · Helibeeld.nl 72, 74 · Lieneke van Hoek 196–198, 199 a. r., 200, 201 · ipv Delft, Henk Snaterse 73, 75–77 · Christopher Frederick Jones 146–148, 149 r. · Hans Jooster 190–195 · Alan Karchmer 119, 121, 123 a. r., 140–145 · Erhard Kargel 14–19, 28–33 · Jos Käser 94–97, 110–113 · Marco Klinger für Sächsische Zeitung 91, 93 r. · Hans-Joachim Kummert 92, 93 l. · Frits van Laar 184 · Jens Lindhe 158–161 · maaars, Zürich 64–67 · Angus Martin Photography 149 l. · Thomas Mayer 34–39 · Sander Meisner, Amsterdam 104–109 · Jeroen Musch 181–183, 185 · Jarosław Naumczyk 40–43 · Jo Pesendorfer, Paris 85 l. · PT Bamboo Pure 162–165 · Matthias Reithmeier 154–157 · Toby Savage 173 · Oliver Schuh+Barbara Burg/www.palladium.de 8–13, 20–23, 150–153 · Marc Verhille 85 r. · Dura Vermeer, Beuningen 199 a. l. · Waterfront Toronto 166–169

Cover front: Alan Karchmer
Cover back (from left to right, from above to below):
CEVM / Foster + Partners / D. Jamme; Christopher Frederick Jones; Jeroen Musch; Oliver Schuh+Barbara Burg/www.palladium.de; AirStudio, Orléans

IMPRINT

The Deutsche Nationalbibliothek lists this publication in the Deutsche Nationalbibliografie; detailed bibliographic data are available in the Internet at http://dnb.dnb.de

ISBN 978-3-03768-175-6
© 2015 by Braun Publishing AG
www.braun-publishing.ch

The work is copyright protected. Any use outside of the close boundaries of the copyright law, which has not been granted permission by the publisher, is unauthorized and liable for prosecution. This especially applies to duplications, translations, microfilming, and any saving or processing in electronic systems.

1st edition 2015

Selection of projects: Editorial office van Uffelen
Editorial staff and layout: Christina Mihajlovski, Lisa Rogers, Johanna Schröder
Graphic concept: Michaela Prinz, Berlin
Reproduction: Bild1Druck GmbH, Berlin

All of the information in this volume has been compiled to the best of the editor's knowledge. It is based on the information provided to the publisher by the architects' and designers' offices and excludes any liability. The publisher assumes no responsibility for its accuracy or completeness as well as copyright discrepancies and refers to the specified sources (architects' and designers' offices). All rights to the photographs are property of the photographer (please refer to the picture credits).